Lázaro Droznes

NEW...DIRTY, FUNNY, SEXY, WITTY ONE LINER JOKES

The best hot one liners to practice oral sex at home or at the office.

Published by UNITEXTO

NEW DIRTY, FUNNY. SEXY, WITTY, ONE LINER JOKES
The best hot one liners to practice oral sex at home or at the office.

Sex without love is empty sex. Even so, it's worth it.

You should live only what you can post on Facebook.

Men disclose their love deeds and women hide them.

Sex is a consequence of genocracy, the government of genes.

In love, we are all self-taught.

The new version of the Barbie doll is promiscuous: she makes love with all the toys.

The future always arrives earlier than planned.

Love is overrated.

Marriages should take a sex insurance policy against third parties.

Talking is the toll paid by men to get t sex.

I had two failed marriages. In the first, my wife left. In the second she stayed.

The problem with knights in a shining armor is that sooner or later it begins to rust.

It is better to be an anonymous alcoholic than a

famous drunk.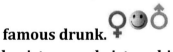

Vices hide virtues and virtues hide vices.

It was love at second sight because the first time I did not know he was rich.

In the Jewish cemetery nobody has the tombs to their name: they all use figureheads.

Bipolar Jews have two states: sales are high or

sales are low.

In time, good women become goddesses and bad women become witches.

Cars must be German and women must be French.

To make love in the car you need good shock absorbers.

The human being is an alchemist: he turns sex into love and love into sex.

I have not failed in love but tried a thousand ways not to be happy.

When a man is rich, women learn to love him.

Husbands are like snails because they think the shell is theirs.

Women sleep with the men who make them dream.

My favorite password is "mypenis", but it gets rejected me because it is too short

Only those who don´t try to be happy fail in love.

82 percent of the statistics on sexual habits are not reliable.

Sexual energy is too valuable to be dedicated to sex.

Since the lamps of low consumption appeared, the lamp of Aladdin went into decay.

My wife ran away with a guy but I'm happy because I made a new friend.

The only justified subsidy is the one you get.

Love is a candle light dinner in a luxurious restaurant. Marriage is a delivery of Chinese food.

Love is caressing on the couch. Marriage is discussing which coach to use.

When in love we lose our appetite, but we recover it after marriage.

Marriage is the most expensive way to have free sex.

Marriage gives us the opportunity to become aware of our shortcomings.

I told my wife that I was going to make her the happiest woman in the world: she replied that she would miss me.

Women take lovers to have a second opinion. Men do it because they do not accept the opinion of their wife.

I have sex once every day. A total of 8 times per week.

Love is ephemeral. Genes are eternal.

Men want a throne and women want an altar.

Of all my addictions, the easiest to quit was my sex addiction.

Women have a problem for every solution their husbands offer.

The Kamasutra is the illustrated version of the Ten Commandments.

Marriage is the bill that comes after love is over.

The most expensive women are those who do not charge.

Prostitutes exist because they are women whose cost is known in advance.

My wife asked for a divorce because she suspected I am not the father of our last child.

He killed his parents and then asked for clemency based on his orphan status.

HOW to HUG is not a self help book. It is the 7h volume of the Encyclopedia Britannica.

The Bible teaches us to love our neighbor and the Kama Sutra shows how to do it.

Judges are good lovers because they make love by the book.

Marriage lasts even if it is expensive, because divorce is much more.

When there is a theft of wigs, the first thing the police do is to comb the area.

Feminists are anorgasmic.

All brides are beautiful and all the dead are good.

The truth is lonely and naked because nobody wants to see it.

God created man first because he did not want a woman to give him advice on how to do it.

When a man marries, he divorces his mother

Men chase the women to recover the rib required for her creation.

Men look at other women to verify how beautiful is theirs.

Women ask questions to receive answers they do not want to hear..

The stewardess was so eager to have a baby that she got pregnant with the autopilot.

When a woman does not give credit to a man, she surrenders for cash

My wife divorce me because she cannot accept that I'm a cuckold.

Women enjoy the wrong man while the right man

arrives.

Lack of sex has two consequences: One is the lack of memory. The other I do not remember.

To fake the orgasm or not to fake? This is the question.

The size matters because men care.

The dead had taken so much Viagra that the undertaker could not close the coffin.

All the jokes about my penis are too short.

How much is the square root of 69?

Booze was developed by ugly women to have sex.

The lightest organ of the body is the penis because it can be lifted with thoughts.

Some celebrate the wedding anniversary. Others

commemorate it.

No woman regrets her orgasms.

She was such a passive woman in bed that she fell asleep

Feminists are femicidal.

The solution for a micro penis is a micro vagina.

My wife screams when she makes love. Especially if I go into the bedroom.

In love, the exchange of ideas leads to the exchange of fluids.

Women have sex to talk. Men talk to have sex.

Crime does not pay except in bed.

I like hard eggs and hard penises

Marriage is a collateral damage of love.

To make good love is essential to practice a lot at home.

I have learned to handle several tongues. Except my wife's.

Marriage is a journey of self-knowledge.

During marriage, the abdomen of the husbands turns from washing board to washing machine.

When I turned 70 I changed my sexual preference and became a vegetarian.

I am not a green old man but a green young man who did not mature.

The main cause of divorce is marriage

I am such a loser that the clerk did not want to sell

me an inflatable doll.

The pink princesses and the blue princes sooner or later fade.

Two actors meet and greet each other: "How am I? All right. And me?

The worst scenario after making love is to hear your woman say: "Dear , you have to paint the ceiling."

Women want to have the same rights as men except when it is time to pay for dinner.

Women fake their weaknesses to hide their strengths.

Every tear of a woman is a crocodile tear.

A man of 80 falls in love with a woman and proposes to her: "Would you like to be my widow?

Husbands come and go. Genes stay.

The positive side of old age is that it cures premature ejaculation.

I promise you I will not make promises.

Children should receive love. Adults should provide it.

Regarding love, I am not superstitious because it brings bad luck

Love at first sight is like lightning. The brightness comes first and then the sound.

If the brain were an app we would use it much more.

Women with short fuses need men with a long penis.

Women fall in love with the vices of men, not their virtues.

I bought an inflatable doll but it turned out to be a lesbian.

No matter how much we study, our ignorance will always be infinite.

Jesus was Jewish because his mother thought he was God.

Catholics ask the Virgin Mary to sin without getting pregnant.

The future is not what it used to be.

If our God continues to disappoint us, we will have to write a New Testament.

The world will be peaceful if peace is more profitable than war.

A doctor's visit is shorter than the quickie of a hurried husband.

You shouldn't judge a crocodile by his teeth.

I miss the days when I had a phallocentric vision of the world.

My dreams are wife's nightmares.

Homosexuality used to be forbidden. Now it's optional. In the future it will be mandatory.

Our marriage advances in ZigZag. When I think it's Zig, my wife thinks it's Zag.

A wife is someone who helps us to solve problems we would not have in case of being single

The porn video was so bad that in the end the couple got married.

Success is like pregnancy. Nobody asks you how many times you got fucked.

▫ Language make love holy at dinner and profane in bed.

Jews do not drink alcohol to be able to better sufferings.

The marriage solves the same problems it generates.

I like marriage, but I'm not fanatical.

There are not erotic books in Braille because the dots get worn out very fast.

Newton discovered the law of gravity when he started having erection problems.

My love for my wife was a false positive.

Confessions of a 90 years old widower: I go out with younger women because I do not get women of my age.

The only way to improve my reputation is to die.

Marriage transforms dreams into nightmares.

Storms are not suspended due to bad weather.

The death of a loved one condemns us to perpetual absence.

Death is normal. Life is an exceptional state.

Some loves affairs leave traces. Others leave scars.

We must not let failure make us dizzy.

So much accusations of sex harassment promote homosexuality.

My father had 4 children. My children have 4 parents.

I'm bipolar- Sometimes I like it and sometimes I do not.

The only men who leave women with their mouths open are dentists.

Adam and Eve were happy because they did not have mothers-in-law.

Adam and Eve were faithful because they had no options.

I stopped buying Viagra because the pills were always expiring.

Masochists never confess when they are under torture.

Religion is the opium of the people. What drug do you use?

The naked white women appear in Playboy. The black white women appear in National Geographic.

The Jews always take advantage. They pay the school for one and learn for three.

When we fulfill our dreams, our nightmares begin.

I need a Jewish boyfriend with Christian virtues.

The mothers-in-law are always in a critical state.

You cannot make surprise parties for fortune tellers.

The tango began between men and then degenerated.

I quit sadomasochism because I always had to be the masochist.

Jews have a reputation for being rich because they always pay for the broken dishes.

A Christian is a Jew after Christ.

Sex is never casual.

Love is an overestimation of the differences between one woman and the other.

Sign on the entrance door of the Nostalgia Club: WE WARN VISITORS THAT THIS CLUB IS NOT WHAT IT USED TO BE

Indecision is also a decision.

There are 2 kinds of women. Those who moan and those who groan.

There are more happy widows than sad ones.

Sex without love is not a good experience. But it is not bad either.

Women are like snails. After enjoying they return to their shell.

I am a masochist with my wife and a sadist with my lover.

Never let failure go to your head

It was a beautiful love story until they got married.

Sex without love is an empty experience. But not too much.

I do not talk about my private life because I do not have any.

Lately, I have more medical appointments than dates.

I am bisexual. The one who is gay is my boyfriend.

Parliament is about to pass a law that makes homosexuality mandatory.

I'm straight. But flexible.

Men are like chewing gum. In the beginning they are sweet. Then they cannot be swallowed and in

the end they get stuck.

When the waters of the Red Sea came down Moses made the decision to buy.

Believing in superstitions brings about bad luck.

Unrequited love lasts forever.

In marriage you have to be optimistic and leave pessimism for better times.

My wife moves with the speed of light to never celebrate her birthdays

When the passengers of Lufthansa adjust the safety belts, a single click is heard.

Young people make love. Old people buy it.

To renew the passion in the couple you have to change one of its members.

According to Jewish mothers life begins when the embryo becomes a doctor.

Money is fungible. So is love

Women watch the porn videos until the end to see if the couple gets married.

Good love is made with long-lasting XXX batteries.

Love should be made like the James Bond martinis: stirred, not shaken.

I am not a sexually disabled person but I do have different abilities

There are two kinds of married women: those having a lover and those looking for one.

Only unrequited love is true love.

Men start as stars and end up as satellites.

For men, paradise is where Eve is. For women, where the apple is.

The secret of having a young woman forever is to send her on a trip at the speed of light and stay still waiting for her to return.

To enjoy the great virtues of a woman it is necessary to forgive her small defects. To enjoy the little virtues of a man it is necessary to forgive his great defects.

Fellatio is one of the Fine Arts.

Good sex, if long, it´s twice as good.

The feminine gender confirms quantum mechanics: the woman is not a certainty but a probability.

People start to die when they quit on desire.

I have issues with my gay boyfriend. We are both passive.

Men cannot fake an erection, but they can fake the relationship.

Women can simulate orgasm. Not the lubrication.

My wife is happy in bed when I do not wake her up.

Before women wanted romance. Now they want orgasms.

Sex is disgusting only when it is done well.

Sex without love is empty sex. Is that a problem?

When women are very horny there are no soft penises.

Life begins with oral sex and ends with written sex.

Sex is what we do while waiting for love.

New penis fucks well.

Gmail is so popular because it lets you quickly to know where the G-spot is.

Good lovers burn but do not get burnt out.

When sex becomes an obligation, the couple becomes a marriage.

Orgasm always pays off.

I am son unlucky in love that my inflatable doll got pregnant.

Polyglots master many tongues, except their wife´s.

Fellatio is an act of domination or submission?

Men keep following the women who take the wrong path.

The exchange of words between man and woman

leads to the exchange of fluids.

Life is the main cause of death.

The highpoint of a Jewish mother is her son winning the Nobel Prize.

I divorced my wife because we could not solve the problems caused by the marriage.

I only regret not having loved my ex-wife well enough.

I only ask God to let me attend my own wake.

Vegetarian food prolongs life ... of cows.

My wife used to ask me to change positions while making love. Now she asks the same, but to stop snoring.

My father was a man of principles. I am a man of endings.

Women dress for women and undress for men.

A new technique of Hindu meditation achieves penile levitation.

I am the only flaw of my wife, but it looks good on her.

My wife is vegetarian. But her vagina is not.

Good lovers do not snore after making love.

The worst sex is the one we do not have.

I did not leave sex. Sex left me.

I'm very good in bed. I can sleep up to 10 hours in a row.

Politics is the second oldest profession in the world. It is very similar to the first.

The problem with mermaids is that it is very difficult to locate their G spot.

Pretty women should be told they are smart, and smart women they are beautiful.

I like good women, but I prefer the bad ones.

Sex is overrated while masturbation is underrated

Men pay for sex because they do not know how to make it.

Our last simultaneous orgasm happened when we signed the divorce papers.

Each woman's wrinkle is an ill-fated orgasm.

There is no life after death. There is before.

Love is like the Moebius ribbon: you do not know if you are up or down.

Women are liberated but not free. They are condemned by their biology.

My kingdom for an erection.

My wife is bipolar. Sometimes she comes and sometimes she does not.

The GPS has been so successful because it is the abbreviation of G POINT SYSTEM.

The real Jewish humor is the one *goym* do not understand.

We the pessimists always say we are realistic.

Every time my wife wants to make love, the system goes down.

When a woman says the magic is over, it means she discovered the trick.

The dreams of the wives are the nightmares of their husbands.

Men are an unnecessary evil.

Marriage is a Jewish invention not pay for sex.

Vicious circles are transformed into love triangles.

The main problem of sex is that it lasts very few minutes.

The favorite prayers of women are: "Oh my God. Keep doing it. For Jesus, do not stop. Thanks for everything."

Women look for a prince and settle for a toad.

Virtuous circles become vicious with a single click.

My wife is like Google; I say two words and she completes the sentence.

A hot woman is like a haunted piano. She plays all alone.

Humor is the portal of love.

The difference between eroticism and pornography is the amount of light in the room.

Our first love is lifelong except when it ends in marriage.

Moses was the first to download documents from the cloud.

The best phrase you can hear while making love is "do not stop"

In Israel, when the low tide comes, everyone buys.

Our present is the future that in the past seemed so uncertain.

It's not here. It's not me. It's not with me.

A good fellatio practitioner never starves.

Good love, if brief, is bad.

The erection is telekinesis because it is done with thought.

I prefer experienced women because they can appreciate what is good.

The son asks his father how much would cost to marry and the father replies: "I do not know, I'm still paying."

Men talk about sex more than they do. Women do the opposite.

Bride and groom celebrate their anniversary. When married they commemorate it.

I am not impotent, just have different sexual skills.

Couples solve the problems they create

Women sleep with the men who let them dream.

The young have premature ejaculation. The old, deferred ejaculation.

When a love story leads to marriage, it is not a happy end.

Manufacturing bottles used to be a blow job.

THE END

Made in United States
North Haven, CT
16 November 2022

26781902R00024